I'm Glad I'm Your DA

written by Bill and Kathy Horlacher

illustrated by Kathryn Hutton

Third Edition, 1996
Library of Congress Catalog Card Number 84-052171
© 1985, The Standard Publishing Company, Cincinnati, Ohio
A division of Standex International Corporation. Printed in U.S.A.

I'm glad I'm your dad!
Please let me say why . . .

I'm glad I'm your dad
when we tickle and hug—

or when we are wrestling
all over the rug.

I'm glad I'm your dad
when we take a nice walk—

or turn off the TV
and just sit and talk.

I'm glad I'm your dad
when you sing me a song—

or when you say "sorry"
if something goes wrong.

I'm glad I'm your dad
when you give me a smile—

or when we build with blocks
for a long, long while.

I'm glad I'm your dad
when I help you get dressed—

or when we play ball,
and you give it your best.

I'm glad I'm your dad
when you pick up your toys—

or when you are able
to hold down the noise.

I'm glad I'm your dad
when you tell me your cares—

or when we are quiet
for you to say your prayers.

I'm glad I'm your dad
when your hurts get better—

or when I'm away,
and you send me a letter.

I'm glad I'm your dad
when we share a good snack—

or when I've been gone,
and you welcome me back.

But most of all,
I'm glad I'm your dad
Just because you're you.

You're God's wonderful gift to me!